SHADOWS OF PROCRASTINATION

Techniques to overcome procrastination and depression

All rights reserved. No part of this publication may be reproduced, distributed, or transmitted in any form or by any means, including photocopying, recording, or other electronic or mechanical methods, without the prior written permission of the publisher, except in the case of brief quotations embodied in critical reviews and certain other noncommercial uses permitted by copyright law.

Copyright© (Lucy Adams) 2024

To my past self,

who taught me resilience and strength,

and to all those who struggle in silence,

may this book light your path forward.

Acknowledgment

I extend my heartfelt gratitude to everyone who supported me in bringing this book to life. Special thanks to:

- My family, for their unwavering love and encouragement.

- My friends, for their patience and understanding during late nights of writing.

- Jane, for her invaluable feedback and constructive criticism.

- The readers, whose stories inspired me to share my own.

Your support has been instrumental in shaping this journey. Thank you."

TABLE OF CONTENT

Acknowledgment
INTRODUCTION
Chapter 1
    Identifying the Shadows
        The Roots of Procrastination
        The Hidden Causes of Depression
        Common Signs of Depression
        Advanced Signs of Depression
        Distinguishing Depression, Laziness, and Procrastination
        Procrastination is Not Laziness
Chapter 2
    The Procrastination-Depression Cycle
        Understanding the Downward Spiral
        Breaking the Downward Spiral
        Understanding Paralysis by Overwhelm
Chapter 3
    Mindset Mastery
        What is Mindset Mastery?
        Building a Mastered Mindset

- Negative Self-Talk
- Positive Affirmations
- Personal Story: My Journey to Mindset Mastery
- Embracing Mistakes as Learning Opportunities

Chapter 4
- Practice Strategies for Action
- Lack of Structure and Its Impact on Life
- Practice Strategies for Action
- Time Management and Its Techniques

Chapter 5
- Role of Physical Health in Mental Clarity
- Exercise and Nutrition for Enhanced Well-being and Motivation
- Nutrition
- Understanding Stress and Strategies for Overcoming It

Chapter 6
- Sustaining Long-Term Change
- Relapsing into Old Patterns
- Solutions to Relapsing
- What is an Unsupportive Environment?

Recap of Key Points
The Way Forward

Shadows of procrastination

INTRODUCTION

Procrastination and depression are two debilitating issues that can deeply affect one's quality of life. They often go hand in hand, creating a vicious cycle that can be difficult to break free from. Let me explain what these terms mean and how they relate to each other.

What is Procrastination?

Procrastination is the act of delaying or postponing tasks or decisions. It's not about being lazy or disorganized; it often arises from deeper psychological factors such as fear of failure, anxiety, or perfectionism.

Procrastinators may avoid tasks because they feel overwhelming, stressful, or boring, opting instead for immediate, easier, or more pleasurable activities. Over time, this habit can lead to significant stress, missed opportunities, and a sense of guilt or failure.

What is Depression?

Depression is a serious mental health condition characterized by persistent feelings of sadness, hopelessness, and a lack of interest or pleasure in activities. It affects how a person feels, thinks, and handles daily activities. Symptoms of depression can include fatigue, changes in sleep and appetite, difficulty concentrating, and even physical pain. Depression can be triggered by various factors, including genetics, trauma, stress, or significant life changes.

The Relationship Between Procrastination and Depression

Procrastination and depression often have a bidirectional relationship, meaning each can contribute to the start and worsening of the other. Here's how they are interconnected:

1. *Procrastination Leading to Depression:* Constantly putting off

tasks can lead to feelings of failure, guilt, and low self-esteem. When important responsibilities are neglected, it can create significant stress and anxiety. Over time, these negative emotions can accumulate, potentially leading to or exacerbating depression.

2. ***Depression Leading to Procrastination:*** Depression can sap a person's energy and motivation, making even simple tasks feel insurmountable. The lack of interest or pleasure in activities, a common symptom of depression, can lead to chronic procrastination. The overwhelming nature of depression can make it difficult to focus or take action, thus perpetuating the cycle.

I was a victim of procrastination and depression back in 2020 when I had nothing to do and I was so broke. All the work I came in contact with couldn't even tend to my feeding, let alone my tuition fees at that time. As one of the major breadwinners in my family, I felt an immense weight on my shoulders. My mum died when I was four, so my dad raised me and my three siblings. The pressure to support my family was overwhelming, and it often felt like I was stuck in a dark, unending tunnel.

The combination of financial stress, family responsibilities, and the loss of my mother contributed to my feelings of hopelessness and helplessness. I found myself avoiding tasks and responsibilities because they felt too overwhelming, which only added to my guilt and frustration. It was a vicious cycle that seemed impossible to break.

A Path Forward

In this book, you will find the techniques I used to overcome procrastination and depression.

Through self-reflection, practical strategies, and a shift in mindset, I was able to step out of the shadows and regain control of my life. I'll share with you the steps I took, the challenges I faced, and the victories I celebrated along the way. My hope is that these techniques will help you, too, find your way out of the darkness and into a life of purpose and fulfillment.

By understanding the relationship between procrastination and depression, and by implementing the strategies outlined in this book, you can begin to break free from the cycle and move towards a brighter, more productive future.

Chapter 1

Identifying the Shadows

The Roots of Procrastination

Procrastination is often misunderstood as mere laziness or a lack of discipline. However, its roots go much deeper, entangling with various psychological and emotional factors. To truly understand procrastination, we need to explore these underlying causes.

One significant root of procrastination is *fear.* This fear can take many forms: fear of failure, fear of success, or even fear of the unknown. When faced with a daunting task, the mind may choose to delay action as a way to avoid potential negative outcomes.

This avoidance provides temporary relief but ultimately leads to increased stress and missed opportunities.

Another common cause of procrastination is *perfectionism.* The desire to perform tasks flawlessly can paralyze individuals, preventing them from starting or completing tasks. The fear of making mistakes or producing superb work can lead to endless delays and self-doubt. Perfectionists often set unrealistically high standards for themselves, making it difficult to take action.

In addition to fear and perfectionism, *emotional* and *psychological* stressors play a crucial role in procrastination. These stressors can be from past traumas, ongoing life challenges, or mental health issues such as anxiety and depression. When the mind is burdened with unresolved emotional pain, it seeks refuge in procrastination as a way to avoid confronting these difficult emotions.

Sarah, a college student, constantly delays working on her assignments. She feels overwhelmed by the pressure to excel academically and fears disappointing her parents, who have high expectations for her. This fear of failure paralyzes her, leading to chronic procrastination. Each time she puts off her work, the anxiety and guilt build up, creating a vicious cycle.

Similarly, James, a young professional, struggles with perfectionism. He spends hours meticulously planning his projects but never feels ready to execute them. His fear of not meeting his own high standards leads to endless procrastination, affecting his productivity and self-esteem. James's procrastination is a way to protect himself from the perceived threat of failure, but it ultimately hinders his progress and success.

For me, the combination of losing my mother at a young age and the subsequent pressure to support my family created a fertile ground for procrastination to grow. The fear of not being able to provide for my siblings and the overwhelming responsibilities made it difficult to take decisive action. Procrastination became a coping mechanism, a way to temporarily escape the weight of my burdens.

Procrastination is not just a habit; it's a complex behavior with deep roots in our emotions and experiences. By identifying these underlying causes, we can begin to understand why we procrastinate and how it affects our lives. Recognizing the role of fear, perfectionism, and emotional stressors is the first step in addressing procrastination and taking control of our actions.

The Hidden Causes of Depression

Depression, like procrastination, has multifaceted and often hidden causes. While it is a deeply personal experience, some common factors contribute to its start. These factors can be ***biological, psychological,*** or *social* in nature, and they often interact in complex ways.

- ***Biologically:*** Depression can be influenced by genetics and brain chemistry. A family history of depression increases the likelihood of experiencing it, as does an imbalance of neurotransmitters in the brain. These chemical imbalances can affect mood, energy levels, and overall mental health.

- ***Psychologically:*** Past traumas and ongoing stressors play a significant role in depression. Experiences such as the loss of a loved one, childhood abuse, or chronic stress can leave lasting emotional scars.

- ***Socially:*** Factors such as isolation, lack of support, and socioeconomic challenges can contribute to depression. Individuals who feel disconnected from others or lack a strong support system are more vulnerable to depressive episodes. Economic hardships, such as job loss or financial instability, can also trigger depression.

John, who recently went through a painful divorce. The emotional trauma of the separation, combined with the stress of adjusting to life as a single parent, led to feelings of loneliness and despair. John's depression was fueled by both the psychological impact of the divorce and the social isolation he experienced as a result.

Similarly, Emma, a middle-aged woman, faced chronic financial difficulties after losing her job. The stress of not being able to make ends meet and the fear of an uncertain future weighed heavily on her. The lack of social support and the ongoing economic strain contributed to her depressive symptoms, making it difficult for her to find hope or motivation.

Common Signs of Depression

1. Persistent sadness or low mood

2. Loss of interest or pleasure in activities once enjoyed

3. Changes in appetite (increased or decreased)

4. Sleep disturbances (insomnia or oversleeping)

5. Fatigue or loss of energy

6. Feelings of worthlessness or excessive guilt

7. Difficulty concentrating or making decisions

8. Irritability or frustration, even over small matters

9. Physical symptoms (headaches, digestive issues, pain)

10. Thoughts of death or suicide

Advanced Signs of Depression

1. Psychomotor agitation or retardation (restlessness or slowed movements)

2. Severe and persistent cognitive impairment

3. Delusions or hallucinations

4. Persistent thoughts of death or suicide attempts

5. Complete withdrawal from social and occupational activities

6. Sleep disturbances, including insomnia or sleeping too much

7. Slowed thinking, speaking or body movements

Distinguishing Depression, Laziness, and Procrastination

Aspect	Depression	Laziness	Procrastination
Emotional State	Persistent sadness, hopelessness	Indifference, lack of enthusiasm	Stress, anxiety, or fear related to tasks
Motivation	Lack of interest or pleasure in activities	Lack of desire to exert effort	Desire to avoid tasks due to fear or overwhelm
Energy Levels	Low energy, fatigue	Often normal but unmotivated	Varies; may have energy but avoid specific tasks
Physical symptoms	Changes in sleep, appetite, and physical pain	Non specific; generally physically fine	May experience stress-related symptoms
Impact on Life	Severe impact on daily functioning	Minimal impact; tends to avoid responsibilities	Can lead to stress and guilt, affecting productivity
Duration	Persistent over weeks or	Ongoing pattern without	Task-specific; may vary in

	months	significant change	duration and intensity
Underlying Causes	Biological, psychological, social factors	Lack of motivation or interest	Fear of failure, perfectionism, anxiety
Behavior	Withdrawal, neglect of responsibilities	Avoidance of effort, preference for inactivity	Delay in starting or completing tasks
Social Interaction	Withdrawal from social activities	May still engage socially but prefers inactivity	May avoid interactions related to pending tasks
Treatment	Professional help, therapy, medication	Behavioral changes, habit formation	Time management, cognitive-behavioral strategies

How They Work Hand in Hand

While depression, laziness, and procrastination are distinct concepts, they can interact in ways that compound their effects. For example, depression can lead to procrastination as individuals struggle with low energy and motivation. Procrastination, in turn, can exacerbate feelings of guilt and worthlessness, worsening depression. Laziness, characterized by a lack of motivation, can sometimes be mistaken for procrastination, though it typically lacks the underlying anxiety and stress.

Procrastination is Not Laziness

Procrastination is often confused with laziness, but they are fundamentally different. Procrastination involves delaying tasks despite knowing the negative consequences, often due to fear of failure, perfectionism, or feeling overwhelmed. Laziness, on the other hand, is a reluctance to exert effort or a preference for inactivity, without the same underlying emotional drivers.

Maria is a dedicated student who frequently finds herself procrastinating on her assignments. She fears that her work won't meet her high standards, so she puts off starting her projects until the last minute. This leads to stress and a sense of failure, despite her commitment to her studies. Maria is not lazy; she's a victim of procrastination driven by her fear of not being good enough.

In contrast, Tom spends most of his free time lounging on the couch and watching TV, even though he has no particular fear or anxiety about tasks. He avoids activities because he simply lacks the motivation to engage in them. Tom's behavior is more aligned with laziness, as it stems from a preference for ease and inactivity rather than a psychological barrier to action.

Shadows of procrastination

Chapter 2

The Procrastination-Depression Cycle

Understanding the Downward Spiral

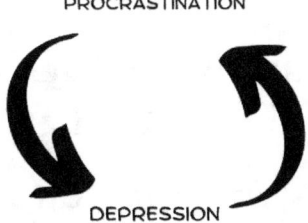

A downward spiral is a self-perpetuating or continuous cycle in which negative behaviors and emotions reinforce each other, leading to progressively worsening outcomes. This concept is often used to describe how mental health issues like depression and anxiety can exacerbate each other or how behaviors like procrastination can lead to increasingly severe consequences.

In the context of procrastination and depression, a downward spiral occurs when each iteration of the procrastination-depression cycle worsens the individual's mental state and ability to cope, making it harder to break free from the cycle.

Characteristics of a Downward Spiral

1. Self-Perpetuating Cycle: Each negative behavior or emotion leads to further negative outcomes, reinforcing the cycle.

2. Progressive Worsening: Over time, the negative effects become more severe and harder to manage.

3. Loss of Control: Individuals may feel increasingly powerless to change their situation.

4. Cumulative Impact: The cumulative effect of each cycle repetition can lead to significant mental, emotional, and physical deterioration.

Examples of Downward Spiral

1. Work-Related Example: Lisa's Project Deadlines

   - *Initial Trigger:* Lisa receives a complex project with a tight deadline at work.

   - *Negative Behavior:* Feeling overwhelmed, she procrastinates, avoiding starting the project.

   - *Short-Term Relief:* Procrastination temporarily alleviates her stress, but the project remains undone.

- *Increased Negative Emotions:* As the deadline approaches, her anxiety and stress increase, leading to feelings of guilt and incompetence.

- *Worsening Condition:* These feelings contribute to depressive symptoms, making it harder for her to concentrate and start the project.

- *Impaired Functioning:* Her productivity decreases, and she misses the deadline, resulting in professional repercussions and further negative emotions.

- *Reinforcement of Cycle:* Each missed deadline worsens her mental state, leading to more procrastination and deeper depression.

2. Home-Related Example: Dave's Household Responsibilities

- *Initial Trigger:* Dave's partner asks him to take on more household responsibilities.

- *Negative Behavior:* Dave feels overwhelmed and starts procrastinating on the chores.

- *Short-Term Relief:* Procrastination gives him temporary relief from the pressure, but the chores pile up.

-*Increased Negative Emotions:* The clutter and undone tasks increase his stress and feelings of inadequacy.

- *Worsening Condition:* This stress contributes to depressive symptoms, such as fatigue and withdrawal.

- *Impaired Functioning:* His ability to manage the household deteriorates, leading to conflicts with his partner and further negative emotions.

- *Reinforcement of Cycle:* Each instance of procrastination deepens his stress and depression, making it harder to take action.

3. School-Related Example: Emily's Study Habits

- *Initial Trigger:* Emily has a challenging upcoming exam.

- *Negative Behavior:* She feels anxious about failing and procrastinates on studying.

- *Short-Term Relief:* Avoiding study reduces her immediate anxiety, but the exam date gets closer.

- *Increased Negative Emotions:* As the exam nears, her anxiety spikes, and she feels guilty for not preparing.

- *Worsening Condition:* The stress leads to depressive symptoms, like hopelessness and lack of motivation.

- *Impaired Functioning:* Her academic performance suffers, and she fails the exam, reinforcing her negative self-view.

- *Reinforcement of Cycle:* Each failed exam heightens her anxiety and depression, leading to more procrastination and academic decline.

Breaking the Downward Spiral

Breaking a downward spiral requires intervention at multiple points in the cycle.

Strategies may include:

1. **Developing Coping Skills:**

Learning stress management and coping techniques to handle triggers effectively.

2. **Setting Realistic Goals:**

Breaking tasks into manageable steps to reduce feelings of overwhelm

3. **Practicing self-love:**

Practicing self-love and reducing self-criticism to mitigate feelings of guilt and worthlessness.

Understanding Paralysis by Overwhelm

Paralysis by overwhelm, also known as overwhelm paralysis, occurs when an individual feels so inundated by the sheer volume or complexity of tasks that they become unable to take any action. This state of being overwhelmed can lead to inaction, where the person feels stuck, unable to decide where to start or how to proceed.

1. **Volume of Tasks**: When faced with a long list of tasks, the brain can become overwhelmed trying to keep track of everything that needs to be done. The person may see a mountain of tasks and feel unsure where to begin.

2. **Complexity of Tasks**: If tasks are perceived as highly complex or difficult, the person may feel inadequate or incapable of completing them, leading to avoidance.

3. **Lack of Clear Direction**: Without a clear plan or priority, the person may

struggle to organize their thoughts and actions, contributing to a feeling of chaos and confusion.

4. **Emotional Reaction**: The stress and anxiety from feeling overwhelmed can cause emotional responses such as panic, fear, or frustration, further inhibiting action.

5. **Cognitive Overload**: The brain can only handle so much information at once. When overloaded, cognitive functions such as decision-making and problem-solving are impaired, leading to a shutdown or freeze response.

Chapter 3

Mindset Mastery

What is Mindset Mastery?

Mindset mastery involves cultivating a positive, resilient, and growth-oriented mindset. It means taking control of your thoughts, beliefs, and attitudes to empower yourself and foster personal growth. A mastered mindset helps you navigate challenges, stay motivated, and achieve your goals. It involves recognizing and shifting negative self-talk, embracing positive affirmations, and developing habits that reinforce a constructive and proactive way of thinking.

Building a Mastered Mindset

1. *Self-Awareness:* Understanding your current mindset and recognizing patterns of negative thinking.

2. *Positive Self-Talk:* Replacing negative thoughts with positive, affirming ones.

3. *Goal Setting:* Defining clear, achievable goals that motivate and guide you.

4. *Continuous Learning:* Accepting challenges as opportunities to learn and grow.

5. *Resilience:* Developing the ability to bounce back from setbacks and view failures as learning experiences.

6. *Gratitude:* Focusing on what you are thankful for to foster a positive outlook.

7. *Visualization:* Imagining your success and the steps needed to achieve it.

Negative Self-Talk

Negative self-talk is the critical inner dialogue that can undermine your confidence and motivation. It often comes from past experiences, fear of failure, or societal pressures.

20 Examples of Negative Self-Talk

1. "I'm not good enough."

2. "I always mess things up."

3. "I can't do anything right."

4. "I'm a failure."

5. "I'll never succeed."

6. "I'm too stupid to figure this out."

7. "Nobody likes me."

8. "I don't deserve happiness."

9. "I'm a burden to others."

10. "I'll never be as good as them."

11. "I always make the wrong decisions."

12. "I can't handle this."

13. "I'm too old/young to change."

14. "It's too late for me."

15. "I'm worthless."

16. "I shouldn't even try."

17. "I'm not talented enough."

18. "I'm always unlucky."

19. "I can't cope with this stress."

20. "Nothing ever goes my way."

Positive Affirmations

Positive affirmations are statements that reinforce positive thinking and self-empowerment. They help shift your mindset from negative to positive, boosting confidence and motivation.

30 Examples of Positive Affirmations

1. "I am capable and strong."

2. "I believe in myself and my abilities."

3. "I am worthy of success and happiness."

4. "I am resilient and can overcome any challenge."

5. "I learn and grow from my experiences."

6. "I am surrounded by love and support."

7. "I choose to focus on the positive."

8. "I am proud of who I am becoming."

9. "I am in control of my thoughts and emotions."

10. "I am grateful for the good in my life."

11. "I am deserving of good things."

12. "I trust myself to make the right decisions."

13. "I am confident in my abilities."

14. "I embrace new opportunities."

15. "I am worthy of love and respect."

16. "I am constantly improving and growing."

17. "I attract positivity and abundance."

18. "I am at peace with who I am."

19. "I am a valuable and unique individual."

20. "I can achieve anything I set my mind to."

21. "I am full of energy and enthusiasm."

22. "I am capable of achieving my goals."

23. "I am kind to myself and others."

24. "I am in charge of my own happiness."

25. "I am a positive thinker."

26. "I am worthy of success."

27. "I handle challenges with grace and strength."

28. "I am open to new ideas and experiences."

29. "I am creative and resourceful."

30. "I am living my best life."

Personal Story: My Journey to Mindset Mastery

I remember vividly, it was a Saturday in August 2023. I was lying on my bed, staring at the ceiling, feeling utterly depressed and sad. I felt helpless and overwhelmed by my circumstances, fantasizing about a life where I was rich and could provide for my family. The missed opportunities and unfulfilled potential sat on my mind.

As I lay there, it struck me that if I continued lying down, crying day after day, year after year, no one was coming to help me. It was up to me to change my life. Immediately, I stood up and picked up a blank book, transforming it into my journal.

I started by writing down the negative self-talk that had plagued me:

- "I'm not good enough."

- "I'll never succeed."

- "I'm a failure."

- "why me?"

I realized these thoughts were holding me back and decided to counter them with positive affirmations:

- "I am capable and strong."

- "I believe in myself and my abilities."

- "I am worthy of success and happiness."

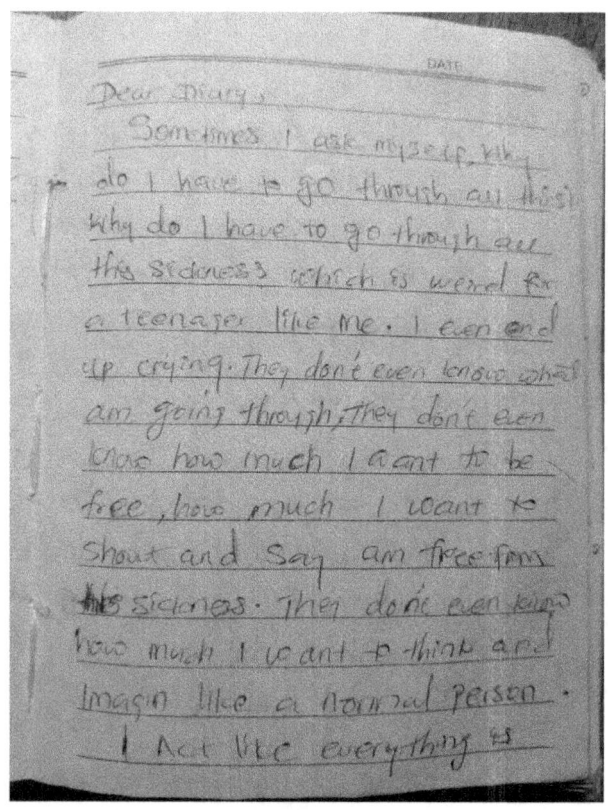

Negative self talk

Shadows of procrastination

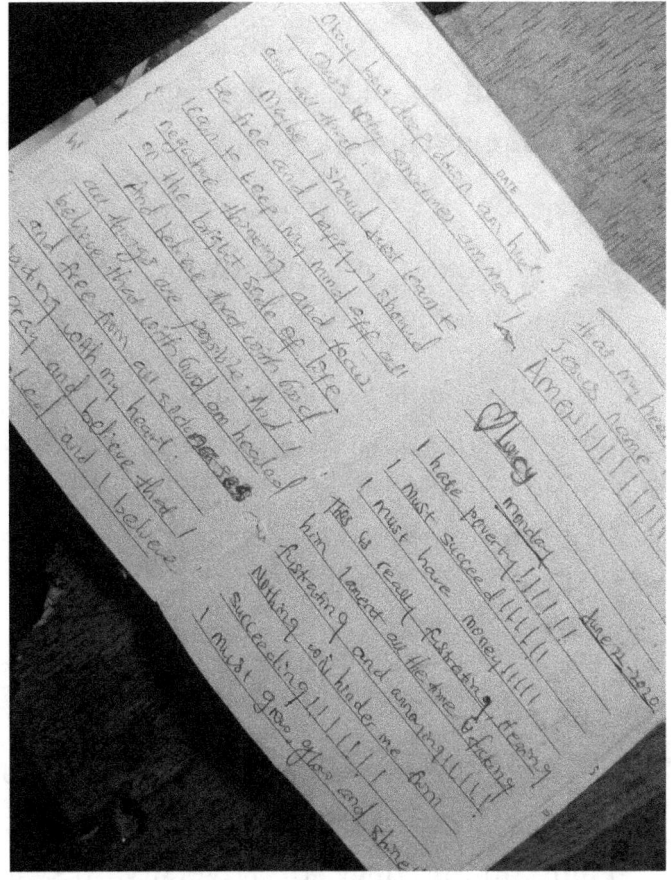

From my diary in 2020

For two weeks straight, I wrote in my journal every day. I documented my negative thoughts and replaced them with positive affirmations. This practice began to change my mindset, helping me see opportunities rather than obstacles. I started to open up my circle, seeking new opportunities and connecting with people who supported my growth.

Through consistent effort and a commitment to positive thinking, I transformed my life.

This chapter is dedicated to helping you do the same by mastering your mindset and tapping in the power of positive self-talk just like I did.

Developing Resilience

Resilience is the ability to bounce back from setbacks, adapt to challenges, and keep going in the face of adversity. It's about maintaining a positive outlook and staying motivated even when things don't go as planned. Developing resilience is crucial for overcoming procrastination and depression, as it empowers you to handle life's inevitable ups and downs with grace and strength.

Embracing Mistakes as Learning Opportunities

It's essential to recognize that mistakes are a natural part of the learning process. Allowing yourself to make mistakes without harsh self-judgment helps build resilience and fosters a growth mindset. When you view mistakes as opportunities to learn and grow, you become more willing to take risks and try new things, which can enhance your productivity and personal development.

How to Learn from Mistakes

1.**Reflect on Your Mistakes:** Take time to analyze what went wrong and why. Understanding the cause of a mistake is the first step to preventing it in the future.

2. **Extract Lessons:** Identify the lessons learned from the mistake. Ask yourself what you can do differently next time to achieve a better outcome.

3. **Implement Changes:** Apply the lessons learned to future tasks. This proactive approach helps you improve and adapt.

4. **Maintain a Positive Attitude:** Focus on the progress you are making rather than dwelling on the mistakes. Celebrate small victories along the way.

Let me tell you all a little story. When I first started out as a writer, I made several mistakes. Even though I loved writing, I often found myself doubting my abilities and fearing failure. My initial attempts were met with criticism and rejection, which made me question my decision to pursue writing.

Despite these setbacks, I decided to use each mistake as a learning opportunity. I took note of the feedback I received and made efforts to improve my skills. I realized that the path to mastery is filled with bumps and that each mistake was a stepping stone to becoming a better writer.

Because I was so broke, I turned to YouTube as a resource for learning. I watched countless videos on writing techniques, storytelling, and even time management. This free resource became my go-to for self-improvement and skill development.

Over time, I saw progress. My writing improved, and I began to feel more confident in my abilities. Even now, I continue to learn and grow because I have come to understand that learning never ends.

This journey taught me the importance of resilience. By allowing myself to make mistakes and learn from them, I became stronger.

Key Takeaways

1. Resilience is Essential: Developing resilience helps you handle setbacks and keep moving forward.

2. Fear of Failure is Detrimental: Overcoming the fear of failure is crucial for improving productivity and reducing procrastination.

3. Embrace Mistakes: View mistakes as learning opportunities rather than failures.

4. Continuous Learning: Always seek opportunities to learn and grow, using available resources like YouTube or other educational platforms.

Chapter 4

Practice Strategies for Action

Lack of Structure and Its Impact on Life

When I was still getting started, one of the biggest challenges I faced was the lack of structure in my life. My days had no clear plan or routine, and I often found myself drifting aimlessly from one task to another without making any real progress. The lack of organization made me feel overwhelmed and anxious, as I could never seem to get anything done.

What is Lack of Structure?

Lack of structure refers to the absence of organized systems, routines, or frameworks in daily life. This can manifest as irregular schedules, undefined goals, chaotic environments, and the absence of planning. Without a structured approach to handling tasks and time, life can become overwhelming and directionless.

How Lack of Structure Affects Life

- ***Increased Stress and Anxiety:*** Lack of organization can create a sense of chaos and unpredictability, leading to heightened stress and anxiety. The uncertainty of not knowing what to do next or how to manage tasks can be mentally exhausting.

- ***Procrastination:*** Without clear plans or schedules, it becomes easier to procrastinate. Tasks are often delayed because there is no clear framework guiding when and how they should be done.

- ***Poor Time Management:*** Structure provides a framework for effective time management. Without it, individuals may struggle to allocate their time efficiently, leading to missed deadlines and rushed tasks.

- ***Negative Impact on Mental Health:*** Constantly dealing with a chaotic and unstructured environment can contribute to feelings of overwhelm, helplessness, and depression. The lack of a clear path can make it difficult to see progress or feel a sense of accomplishment.

- ***Strained Relationships:*** Lack of structure can affect personal and professional relationships. Missed appointments, forgotten commitments, and an inability to manage time effectively can strain relationships and erode trust.

- ***Hindered Goal Achievement:*** Goals require a structured approach to be achieved. Without structure, setting and working towards goals can become difficult, leading to stagnation and a lack of progress.

- ***Reduced Self-Esteem:*** Continually failing to meet obligations or complete tasks due to a lack of structure can lead to feelings of inadequacy and diminished self-esteem.

Examples of Lack of Structure and Its Effects

Work Example:

Imagine you have a job that involves multiple projects with tight deadlines. Without a structured approach to managing your tasks, you might start working on one project only to switch to another without completing the first. This constant switching not only reduces productivity but also increases the likelihood of missing deadlines and producing subpar work. The resulting stress and anxiety can make it difficult to focus and further compound the problem.

Home Example:

At home, a lack of structure can lead to a chaotic environment. If household chores, meals, and family activities are not planned, things can quickly become disorganized. This disorganization can create a stressful atmosphere, making it difficult for family members to relax and enjoy their time together. It can also lead to conflicts as responsibilities are neglected or forgotten.

School Example:

For students, a lack of structure can be particularly detrimental. Without a study schedule, homework, and study sessions can be sporadic and ineffective. This can lead to falling behind in coursework, poor academic performance, and increased stress. The lack of a structured routine can also interfere with developing good study habits and time management skills that are crucial for future success.

Practice Strategies for Action

What Are Practice Strategies for Action?

Practice strategies for action are systematic approaches designed to help you move from intention to execution. These strategies enable you to take consistent, purposeful steps toward your goals, overcoming inertia and breaking the cycle of procrastination. By implementing practical strategies for action, you can turn your plans into reality and make steady progress in various areas of your life.

Practical Strategies for Action

1. Set Clear Goals: Define specific, measurable, achievable, relevant, and time-bound (SMART) goals to give your actions direction and purpose.

2. Break Tasks into Smaller Steps: Divide large tasks into smaller, manageable parts to make them less overwhelming and easier to start.

3. Prioritize Tasks: Rank tasks by importance and urgency to focus on what matters most and avoid getting sidetracked by less critical activities.

4. Create a Schedule: Plan your day, week, or month in advance, allocating specific times for each task to ensure you stay on track. You can make your schedule and put it up on the refrigerator door or on the wall in your room.

5. Use a To-Do List: Write down tasks to keep track of what needs to be done and enjoy the satisfaction of checking them off as you complete them.

6. Set Deadlines: Assign deadlines to tasks to create a sense of urgency and motivation to complete them.

7. Eliminate Distractions: Identify and remove distractions from your environment to maintain focus and productivity.

8. Use the Pomodoro Technique: Work in short, focused intervals (usually 25 minutes) followed by a brief break to maintain high levels of productivity.

9. Reward Yourself: Celebrate your achievements, no matter how small, to maintain motivation and positive reinforcement.

I began using these practical strategies for action, and they helped me immensely.

Setting clear goals and breaking them into smaller steps made them more achievable. Prioritizing tasks and creating a schedule gave me structure and direction. Writing to-do lists and setting deadlines kept me accountable and motivated.

Eliminating distractions and using the Pomodoro Technique improved my focus and productivity even though it was hard because I love watching movies so much. Rewarding myself for completing tasks kept my spirits high. These strategies transformed my approach to daily tasks and gave me a helping hand.

Time Management and Its Techniques

Time management is the process of planning and exercising conscious control over the amount of time spent on specific activities to increase effectiveness, efficiency, and productivity. Good time management enables you to accomplish more in less time, reduces stress, and leads to career success and personal satisfaction.

Time Management Techniques

1. Prioritize Your Tasks: Use methods like the Eisenhower Matrix to categorize tasks based on urgency and importance.

2. Create a Daily Schedule: Plan your day in advance, allocating specific times for each task to ensure you stay on track.

3. Set Goals and Deadlines: Establish clear goals and deadlines for tasks to create a sense of urgency and focus.

4. Use a Planner or Calendar: Keep track of appointments, deadlines, and tasks in a planner or digital calendar.

5. Time Blocking: Allocate blocks of time for specific tasks or activities to maintain focus and productivity.

6. Avoid Multitasking: Focus on one task at a time to ensure better quality and efficiency.

7. Use Technology Wisely: Utilize apps and tools for task management, reminders, and scheduling, but avoid unnecessary digital distractions.

8. Take Breaks: Schedule regular breaks to rest and recharge, maintaining overall productivity and preventing burnout.

9. Delegate Tasks: Delegate tasks to others when possible to free up your time for higher-priority activities.

10. Reflect and Adjust: Regularly review your progress and adjust your strategies as needed to improve time management.

Chapter 5

Role of Physical Health in Mental Clarity

Physical health plays a crucial role in maintaining mental clarity and cognitive function. When our bodies are healthy and well-nourished, our brains function optimally, enhancing focus, memory, and decision-making abilities. Conversely, neglecting physical health can lead to fatigue, brain fog, and reduced mental acuity, making it harder to stay motivated and productive.

Problems Associated with Neglecting Physical Health

1. Decreased Energy Levels: Poor physical health often results in low energy levels, making it difficult to stay alert and focused throughout the day.

2. Increased Stress and Anxiety: Neglecting physical health can exacerbate stress and anxiety, impacting emotional well-being and increasing the likelihood of procrastination.

3. Impaired Cognitive Function: Lack of exercise and proper nutrition can impair cognitive function, affecting memory, learning ability, and decision-making skills.

4. Weakened Immune System: Poor physical health weakens the immune system, making individuals more susceptible to illnesses that can disrupt productivity and well-being.

5. *Sleep Disturbances:* Lack of exercise and poor nutrition can contribute to sleep disturbances, further impacting energy levels and mental clarity.

6. *Mood Swings:* Imbalances in physical health can lead to mood swings, making it challenging to maintain a positive mindset and motivation.

7. *Weight Management Issues:* Neglecting physical health often leads to weight management problems, which can affect self-esteem and overall emotional well-being.

8. *Reduced Resilience:* Physical health influences resilience to stress and adversity.

Neglecting it may decrease resilience, making it harder to bounce back from setbacks.

9. Chronic Health Conditions: Long-term neglect of physical health increases the risk of developing chronic health conditions that can further impact daily functioning and well-being.

10. Impact on Relationships: Poor physical health can strain relationships due to decreased energy, mood disturbances, and overall well-being issues.

Solutions to Enhance Physical Health

1. Regular Exercise: Add regular physical activity into your routine, such as walking, jogging, yoga, or strength training, to improve fitness levels and overall health.

2. Balanced Nutrition: Eat a well-balanced diet rich in fruits, vegetables, lean proteins, and whole grains to provide essential nutrients for energy and brain function.

3. Adequate Hydration: Drink plenty of water throughout the day to stay hydrated and support bodily functions, including cognitive performance.

4. Sufficient Sleep: Prioritize adequate sleep (7-9 hours per night for adults) to enhance cognitive function, mood regulation, and overall health.

5. Stress Management: Practice stress-reducing techniques such as meditation, deep breathing, or hobbies to manage stress levels effectively.

6. Regular Health Check-ups: Schedule regular check-ups with healthcare professionals to monitor physical health indicators and address any concerns promptly.

7. Limit Sedentary Behavior: Reduce prolonged sitting by taking breaks to stretch, walk, or engage in light activity throughout the day.

8. Social Connection: Maintain social connections and support networks, as they play a vital role in emotional and physical well-being.

9. Mindfulness Practices: Put mindfulness practices into your daily routine to promote awareness, reduce stress, and enhance mental clarity.

10. Goal Setting: Set achievable goals related to physical health, such as weight management or fitness milestones, to stay motivated and track progress.

Exercise and Nutrition for Enhanced Well-being and Motivation

Exercise

1. **Brisk Walking:** Improves cardiovascular health and boosts mood.

2. **Cycling:** Builds leg strength and enhances endurance.

3. **Yoga:** Increases flexibility, reduces stress, and promotes relaxation.

4. **Swimming:** Provides a full-body workout with low impact on joints.(PS. Not knowing how to swim is not an excuse, you can begin with any other activity that is listed in this book).

5. Dancing: Combine exercise with fun and improves coordination.

Nutrition

1. Leafy Greens: Rich in vitamins and antioxidants for overall health.

2. Lean Proteins: Supports muscle growth, repair, and satiety.

3. Whole Grains: Provides sustained energy and essential nutrients.

4. Healthy Fats: Supports brain function and reduces inflammation.

5. Fruits and Berries: High in vitamins, minerals, and fiber for overall health.

For the sake of nutrition and for the fact that we are talking about healthy living...

Let me talk about a personal experience of mine and the steps I took towards healing.

ULCER.. yup you had it right. Upon all the struggles I was facing they had to top it with ulcer.

Managing Ulcer with Cabbage Juice:

Living with ulcers can be quite a challenge, but I found a surprisingly effective remedy (A close friend of mine actually told me) that not only helps relieve the pain but also boosts productivity without making me feel like I'm at death's door. Yes, you guessed it right—it's cabbage juice! Let me take you through my journey with ulcer and how cabbage juice became my unexpected savior.

Ulcers are no laughing matter. They can cause persistent pain, discomfort, and sometimes even lead to serious complications if not managed properly. As someone who battles with ulcer, I know firsthand how disruptive it can be to daily life. Whether it's the burning sensation after a meal or the dreaded flare-ups during stressful times, finding relief is crucial.

I stumbled upon an age-old remedy—cabbage juice. Now, before you cringe at the thought of drinking something green and leafy, let me assure you, cabbage juice is surprisingly palatable and packed with healing properties.

How Cabbage Juice Helps

Cabbage is rich in antioxidants and compounds that help protect the stomach lining and promote healing. It has anti-inflammatory properties that can soothe irritated tissues and reduce pain associated with ulcers. Plus, it's a great source of vitamins C and K, which support overall health and well-being.

I must admit, when I first heard about cabbage juice, I couldn't help but laugh at the idea of drinking it, until I almost died three times. But desperate times call for desperate measures, and after a few sips, I realized it wasn't as bad as I imagined. In fact, it quickly became part of my routine, providing relief and even a few chuckles along the way.

Now, let's get down to the nitty-gritty—how to make cabbage juice that not only relieves pain but also tastes surprisingly good:

Ingredients:

- 1 small head of green cabbage

- Water (as needed for blending)

Instructions:

1. Prepare the Cabbage: Wash the cabbage thoroughly and remove any outer leaves that are wilted or damaged.

2. Chop It Up: Cut the cabbage into small pieces to make blending easier and quicker.

3. Blend Away: Place the chopped cabbage into a blender or food processor. Add a bit of water to facilitate blending and blend until smooth.

4. Strain (Optional): For a smoother juice, strain the blended cabbage pulp through a fine-mesh sieve or cheesecloth. Press down on the pulp to extract as much juice as possible.

5. Enjoy Your Juice: Pour the freshly made cabbage juice into a glass and drink it immediately. You can add a touch of honey to enhance the taste if desired.

Not only does cabbage juice help alleviate ulcer pain, but it also boosts productivity by providing essential nutrients and promoting digestive health. When my stomach feels calm and settled, I can focus better on my tasks without the distraction of discomfort.

So there you have it—an effective remedy for managing ulcer pain and enhancing productivity. Cabbage juice may not be the miracle cure for everyone, but it has certainly made a difference in my life. Give it a try and see how it works for you. Who knows, you might find yourself laughing all the way to better digestive health!

Disclaimer:

This is based on personal experience, so make sure you consult your doctor before taking anything that involves your health. Remember, health is wealth.

By prioritizing physical health through exercise, nutrition, and stress management, individuals can enhance mental clarity, boost motivation, and reduce the barriers that contribute to procrastination. Incorporating these strategies into daily life fosters resilience, improves productivity, and supports overall well-being, empowering individuals to achieve their goals.

Understanding Stress and Strategies for Overcoming It

Stress is an inevitable part of life that affects everyone at some point. Understanding its triggers, effects, and effective coping strategies is crucial for maintaining emotional and physical well-being.

Triggers of Stress

Stress can be triggered by a variety of factors, both external and internal. Recognizing these triggers is the first step toward managing stress effectively. Here are eight common triggers:

1. Work Pressure: High workloads, tight deadlines, and job insecurity can lead to significant stress.

2. Financial Concerns: Money problems, debt, and financial instability can cause persistent stress and anxiety.

3. Relationship Issues: Conflict with family members, friends, or romantic partners can be a source of emotional stress.

4. Health Problems: Chronic illnesses, injuries, or concerns about one's health can cause stress.

5. Major Life Changes: Events such as moving, divorce, bereavement,death of a loved one, or starting a new job can be stressful.

6. Uncertainty and Lack of Control: Feeling uncertain about the future or lacking control over circumstances can induce stress.

7. Environmental Factors: Noise, pollution, and overcrowding can contribute to stress levels.

8. Internal Pressures: Perfectionism, self-criticism, and unrealistic expectations can create internal stress.

Negative Reactions to Stress

When faced with stress, individuals may react in ways that are harmful to their well-being. These reactions can increase stress levels and contribute to further difficulties. Common negative reactions to stress include:

1. Avoidance: Ignoring or procrastinating on tasks or responsibilities, which can lead to increased stress over time.

2. Substance Abuse: Turning to alcohol, drugs, or other substances as a coping mechanism.

3. Emotional Outbursts: Reacting with anger, frustration, or irritability towards oneself or others.

4. Isolation: Withdrawing from social interactions and support networks, which can worsen feelings of loneliness and stress.

5. Overeating or Undereating: Using food as a way to cope with stress, can lead to unhealthy eating habits and physical health issues.

6. Sleep Disturbances: Insomnia or oversleeping due to heightened stress levels, can impact overall well-being.

7. Self-Neglect: Ignoring self-care routines such as hygiene, exercise, and relaxation, can further deplete physical and emotional resilience.

8. Cognitive Distortions: Engaging in negative self-talk or catastrophic thinking patterns that exaggerate the stressor's impact.

Overwhelming Stress and Its Impact

Overwhelming stress occurs when individuals are unable to cope with the demands placed upon them. This type of stress can lead to a range of physical, emotional, and behavioral symptoms, including:

- *Physical Symptoms:* Headaches, muscle tension, fatigue, digestive issues, and compromised immune function.

- *Emotional Symptoms:* Anxiety, depression, mood swings, irritability, and feelings of overwhelm.

- ***Behavioral Symptoms:***Procrastination, avoidance behaviors, increased substance use, and difficulty concentrating.

Solutions and Techniques for Managing Overwhelming Stress

1. Mindfulness and Meditation

2. Deep Breathing Exercise

3. Progressive Muscle Relaxation (PMR)

4. Physical Activity

5. Healthy Coping Strategies

6. Time Management

7. Nutrition and Hydration

8. Sleep Hygiene

Chapter 6

Sustaining Long-Term Change

Building habits that last is crucial for maintaining progress. We'll explore how to build these habits, what happens when we relapse into old patterns, and how to get back on track when we do. Spoiler alert: I'm not perfect either, and I've had my fair share of setbacks. But with the right strategies, we can all make lasting changes.

Building Habits That Last

Creating lasting habits is more than just willpower. It involves understanding how habits work and using that knowledge to our advantage. Here's how you can build habits that stick:

1. Start Small: Begin with small, manageable changes. Instead of overhauling your entire routine, focus on one tiny habit. For example, if you want to exercise more, start with a five-minute workout each day.

2. Be Consistent: Consistency is key. Aim to perform your new habit at the same time each day to create a routine. This regularity helps reinforce the behavior and makes it easier to stick with. I know it's not easy but we have to try.

3. Use Triggers: Identify cues that will trigger your new habit. For example, if you want to read more, place a book next to your bed and read a few pages before sleeping.

4. Reward Yourself: Positive reinforcement helps solidify new habits. Give yourself a small reward when you complete your new habit, like a treat or a few minutes of leisure activity.

5. Track Your Progress: Keep a journal or use an app to track your progress. Seeing your progress over time can be motivating and help you stay committed.

6. Stay Flexible: Life happens, and it's important to be flexible. If you miss a day, don't beat yourself up. Simply get back on track the next day.

7. Visualize Success: Spend a few minutes each day visualizing yourself successfully performing your new habit. This mental rehearsal can strengthen your commitment.

8. Make It Enjoyable: Find ways to make your new habit enjoyable. If you enjoy the activity, you're more likely to stick with it.

9. Be Patient: Building new habits takes time. Be patient with yourself and celebrate small victories along the way.

Relapsing into Old Patterns

Even with the best intentions, relapsing into old habits can happen. Trust me, I've been there. There were times when I thought I had my procrastination beat, only to find myself binge-watching TV instead of working. It's important to understand that relapse is a normal part of the change process.

Let me tell you about a time I relapsed. I remember vividly that I had set up this amazing schedule to write every morning. For a while, it was going great. But then, life happened. One particularly stressful week, I skipped a day. Then another. Before I knew it, I was back to my old procrastinating ways, feeling guilty and defeated.

But here's the thing: relapsing doesn't mean failure. It's an opportunity to learn and grow. I realized that I needed to adjust my approach and find better ways to manage stress without falling back into old habits.

Solutions to Relapsing

1. Acknowledge It: The first step is to acknowledge the relapse without judgment. Understand that it's a natural part of the process.

2. Analyze the Trigger: Identify what triggered the relapse. Was it stress, boredom, or something else? Understanding the trigger can help you address it in the future.

3. Recommit to Your Goal: Reaffirm your commitment to the habit. Remind yourself why it's important and how it benefits you.

4. Adjust Your Strategy: Sometimes, a relapse is a sign that your initial strategy needs tweaking. Maybe you need a different trigger, a better reward, or more support.

5. Seek Support: Talk to a friend or mentor about your relapse. They can offer encouragement and help you get back on track.

6. Practice Self-Compassion: Be kind to yourself. Everyone makes mistakes. What matters is how you respond to them.

7. Take Small Steps: Don't try to overhaul everything at once. Take small steps to get back on track.

8. Learn from the Experience: Use the relapse as a learning opportunity. What can you do differently next time to prevent it?

Laughing at your mistakes and mishaps can make the process more enjoyable and less daunting.

What is an Unsupportive Environment?

An unsupportive environment is one that hinders your efforts to make positive changes and build lasting habits. This environment can be physical, social, or emotional. It includes the people, places, and situations that negatively influence your progress and make it difficult to stick to your goals.

Examples of an unsupportive environment include:

1. Negative Social Circles: Friends or family members who discourage your efforts or belittle your goals.

2. Toxic Workplaces: Job environments that are stressful, demanding, or lack positive reinforcement.

3. Distracting Living Spaces: Homes filled with clutter, noise, or distractions that prevent focus and productivity.

4. Critical Parents: Parents who constantly criticize or doubt your abilities and decisions, making you question yourself.

5. Peers Who Procrastinate: Being surrounded by people who have similar procrastination habits can reinforce your own tendencies.

6. Lack of Access to Resources: Environments where you don't have access to the tools, information, or support you need to succeed.

Example 1: Critical Parents

Imagine you're trying to establish a new study routine to improve your grades. However, your parents constantly criticize your efforts, questioning your ability to succeed and reminding you of past failures or worse comparing you to other kids your age. Their negativity makes it hard for you to stay motivated and focused.

Example 2: Toxic Workplaces

You've decided to adopt a healthier lifestyle, including regular exercise and balanced meals. Unfortunately, your workplace is highly stressful, with long hours and little regard for work-life balance. This environment makes it challenging to maintain your new habits.

Example 3: Distracting Living Spaces

You're working from home and trying to stick to a productive schedule. However, your living space is cluttered, noisy, and filled with distractions like a constantly blaring TV or family members who interrupt you frequently. This environment hinders your ability to focus and be productive.

Solutions for Dealing with an Unsupportive Environment

1. Set Boundaries: Communicate your needs and set clear boundaries with those around you. Let them know what you're trying to achieve and ask for their support or at least their respect for your efforts.

2. Create a Positive Space: Transform your physical environment into one that supports your goals. This might mean organizing your workspace, finding a quiet spot to focus, or creating a dedicated area for exercise.

3. *Limit Negative Interactions:* Reduce the time you spend with people who are unsupportive or negative. Instead, seek out positive and encouraging individuals who uplift you.

4. *Seek Support Elsewhere:* If your immediate environment is unsupportive, look for support outside. Join online communities, support groups, or find a mentor who can provide the encouragement and advice you need.

5. *Stay Focused on Your Goals:* Remind yourself regularly why you started and what you hope to achieve. Keeping your goals in mind can help you stay motivated despite external challenges.

6. *Practice Self-Care:* Taking care of your physical and mental well-being can make it easier to cope with an unsupportive environment. Regular exercise, healthy eating, and mindfulness practices can boost your resilience.

7. Develop a Strong Inner Circle: Surround yourself with a few trusted individuals who believe in you and your goals. Their support can make a significant difference.

8. Communicate Openly: Sometimes, people are unaware of how their behavior affects you. Having an honest conversation about your needs and goals can lead to better understanding and support.

9. Use Negative Energy as Motivation: Turn the negative energy from an unsupportive environment into motivation to prove doubters wrong. Channel that energy into your efforts and let it drive you to succeed.

10. Adjust Your Environment: If possible, make changes to your environment. This might mean rearranging your living space, finding a new job, or relocating to a place that better supports your goals.

As we reach the conclusion of this book, it's time to step out of the shadows and into the light of a brighter, more productive future. Let's recap our journey.

Recap of Key Points

1. Understanding Procrastination and Depression:

- We began by defining procrastination and depression and examining how they are interconnected. We discussed how procrastination can fuel depression, creating a downward spiral that can be difficult to break.

2. Identifying the Shadows:

- We explored the root causes of procrastination, such as fear of failure, perfectionism, and lack of motivation. We also looked at how personal experiences, like the loss of a loved one or being thrust into responsibility at a young age, can contribute to these issues.

3. Mindset Mastery:

- In Chapter 3, we discussed the importance of mastering your mindset. This included recognizing and combating negative self-talk, using positive affirmations, and developing a resilient attitude to handle setbacks.

4. Developing Resilience:

- We highlighted the importance of resilience in overcoming procrastination and depression. We shared stories and strategies for bouncing back from mistakes and learning from them, reinforcing that making mistakes is a natural part of the growth process.

5. Practice Strategies for Action:

- We provided practical strategies for taking action, including time management techniques and ways to maintain focus and productivity. We also discussed the importance of having a structured routine to avoid falling back into old habits.

6. Sustaining Long-Term Change:

- Finally, we explored how to sustain long-term change by building lasting habits, dealing with relapses, and creating a supportive environment. We discussed strategies for maintaining motivation and staying committed to your goals.

The Way Forward

As you move forward, remember that the journey to overcoming procrastination and depression is ongoing. It requires continuous effort, self-awareness, and the willingness to adapt and grow. Here are some steps to keep in mind:

1. Set Clear Goals

2. Stay Consistent

3. Be Patient and Kind to Yourself

4. Seek Support

5. Continue Learning and Adapting

As we conclude this book, I want to remind you that you are not alone in this journey. Many people struggle with procrastination and depression, but with determination and the right strategies, you can overcome these challenges just like I did.

Remember, it's okay to stumble and fall. What matters most is how you pick yourself up and keep moving forward. Accept your imperfections and view each setback as an opportunity to learn and grow.

You have the power to transform your life. By applying the techniques and insights shared in this book, you can step out of the shadows of procrastination and depression and into a future filled with purpose and productivity.

So, take that first step. Make a commitment to yourself to keep pushing forward, no matter how difficult it may seem. You are capable of achieving great things, and your journey is just beginning.

And as you continue on this journey, I have some exciting news! I'm currently working on a new fiction book. Stay alert for its release, and I would love for you to review it and give me your honest feedback. Don't forget to check back once in a while to see if Lucy Adams has written a new book. I can't wait to see you in my other works!

Thank you for allowing me to be a part of your journey. I believe in you, and I know you have the strength and resilience to overcome any obstacle that comes your way. Here's to a brighter, more fulfilling future—one step at a time.

With hope and determination,

Lucy Adams.

P.S. If you thought cabbage juice was the secret weapon, wait until you see what I have in store for you next!

FROM THE AUTHOR

THESE SHADOWS

Shadow work and gratitude journal - prompts and activities for healing and growth with guided workbook

Interesting fun facts for smart kid

PERFECT ESCAPE

How to safely escape an abusive relationship

www.ingramcontent.com/pod-product-compliance
Lightning Source LLC
Chambersburg PA
CBHW071942210526
45479CB00002B/780

I made an exact replica of the meal plan I used in my procrastination journey and the weight loss template I drew out for my friend Emma, which she used in her weight loss journey.

Shadows of procrastination